METAMORPHOSIS OF JOY

Albert Dépas

METAMORPHOSIS OF JOY

Text and Artwork by Albert Depas

Foreword by Barry Wallenstein

Copyright 1996 by Albert Depas

All rights reserved. No part of this book may be reproduced or transmitted in any form or by any means - graphic, electronic, or mechanical, including photocopying, recording, or any information storage or retrieval system - for sale without written permission from the publisher, except quotations included in a review.

Published by:

Mega Press
P.O. Box 172
New York, NY 10009
(212) 560-2439

Library of Congress Catalog Card Number: 96-94500
ISBN # 0-9651473-0-4

Printed and bound in the United States of America
by Mirror Image Printing & Graphics Inc.

Cover design and artwork by Albert Depas

All illustrations are by Albert Depas

Photo of the Author by Hsuan-Tsun Kuo

DEDICATION

This book of poetry
is dedicated to all
who love without envy,
forgive without regrets,
and have a great desire
to live in harmony
with everyone.

ACKNOWLEDGEMENTS

The production of this book was made possible with the help of many close friends and associates. To those individuals I am very thankful. I wish to acknowledge some people for their specific duties: Jackie Winslow for typing and correcting the manuscript, Carol Segarra for typesetting and layout, Charity Hume and Barry Wallenstein for their most valuable editorial advice and most of all Meg Feeley. I wish to mention also the publications in which some of these poems were published: *Poetry in Performance, Wheel-Work, Painters as Poets, Poetry For An Open Mind, Fifth Floor* and *Show & Tell.*

CONTENTS

Foreword by Barry Wallenstein

9 **Part I: Burdened Reality**

11 The Dark Side Of Me
12 Miss Opportunitie
14 Fulfillment And Desire
16 Drug Addicts
18 Excuses! Excuses!
19 Senseless Desires
20 Bridges
22 Business Talk
23 Being Legal
24 Burdened Reality

25 **Part II: Confrontation**

27 Sibling Rivalry
28 Daddy's Way
30 Trick Or Treat
31 Kissing Death
32 Confrontation

33 **Part III: Metamorphosis Of Joy**

35 Take Off From A Relationship
36 A Friendly Memo
37 Paolina
38 Mystery Lady
40 Seven Hearts Angel
42 Fools In Love
44 Metamorphosis Of Joy
46 Joy

47	**Part IV: My Book**
49	No Origin
50	A Puzzle Within
51	Talking Art
52	Right Of Purpose #1
53	Right Of Purpose #2
54	An Endless Walk
56	Beyond The Horizon
57	Truth 101
58	A Pensive Moment
60	On And On
61	My Book
64	Bio

FOREWORD

Albert Depas, the speaker, editor, painter, and encourager of the arts, here metamorphoses his voice from talker to singer as his diction transforms from commonplace expression to the highly charged forms of poetic speech. One of the many pleasures of this book, Mr. Depas' first, is the way his poetry records shifting perspectives, from joy to the expression of loss or doubt, from the dogged optimism of the title poem to those less certain poems which engage us in darker moods. In one poem he speaks of "the nagging/of achievement"; the quest throughout these poems—for identity, love or simply well-being—is the achievement.

If joy were not to metamorphose, how would it treat us finally? I imagine a dulled state with no striving. Changing joy into other states of awareness, the poet provides us with the real world, maybe less easily sung about, but convincing when deeply felt:

> Silently, I sat like a pile of socks,
> then sweetly, in my corner,
> the birds sang.
> My legs were tight
> as if they were in stocks.
> I could not dance or sing.
> So I banged.

At the heart of change is the wish to change. Poetry itself is the record of change within the writer, the turning of a wish into a form or pattern of words, an act that rejuvenates pleasure. Many of Depas' poems play on the border of ritual, with wishes: "Wishing wishes/with wishbones/hanging by my neck/I am soon to find/my wish."

The persona is a city dweller who needs to be "reassured" of his "own territory," physical and psychic. He is often on shifting ground where he wonders in the midst of sensual pleasure "why she didn't go?" It is the wounded, sometimes drifting, sensibility searching for solidity and then strategies to heal the pain or decipher the dilemma — the path to current discomforts. In addition to the individual's isolation in the urban environment, these also include his relationship to the city or the state by way of taxes, the legal system, and the family. Read especially the discomforting "Daddy's Way."

Humor is a principal device used to deflect the currents of uncertainty, the feeling of being "displaced" by love or death. A section near the end of "Fulfillment and Desire" involves us in a positive world, unburdened by the suffering ego of anyone behind this poem.

> And in no time fulfillment
> grabs my legs and sets the hinges straight
> as if they were part of my hip bones.
> I get up, catch my breath
> and feel as if I've been
> on a rescue mission.

Elsewhere he says "Whether it's monkey business or not/business is business." The urge to lighten up brightens these very serious poems.

Barry Wallenstein

Part I
Burdened Reality

THE DARK SIDE OF ME

*The dark side of me
is buried into the light
that others do not see;
a mirrored image
of black matter from the universe;
rays piercing through
the ignorant, arrogant egotist
of those claiming to be righteous.*

*The dark side of me,
dark as the midday sun
of the summer solstice
stands high while others run
with a shameful, bigoted notice.*

*The dark side of me
sits calmly as a prism
separating the wisdom
of ancient days
from the cracking noise
of eroded wisdom teeth.*

*Though the dark side of me
is as dark as a mystery
yet to be conceived,
the bright light of others,
in its pseudo-perception,
finds its sustenance
from the core of my darkness.*

MISS OPPORTUNITIE

*Miss Opportunitie came to see me once,
at the awakening of the sun.
I was too young to be gentle
and embrace her:
lack of experience coupled
with little light to see.*

> *She then moved on,
> or returned to...
> Who knows where?*

*She came a second time.
It was noon time,
with blinding light.
And Experience having being
too busy and full of energy,
couldn't care much to even let me
wink a blink in her direction.*

> *She then moved on,
> or returned to...
> Who knows where?*

Another time,
at the setting sun time;
while I was napping
I had an overlapping thought.

    Miss Opportunitie!

    She returned to...
    Who knows where?

Again when she comes,
I shall caress her
into napping on my lap.
Then we'll snore and dream together
even have wet dreams
or nightmares, I don't care.

I'll hold her on my lap
'til I awake
to see her eye to eye,
and communicate
my most delicate thoughts to her:
less experience denied
and vandalizing energy.

FULFILLMENT AND DESIRE

*At the Grace Hope Mission
and the Peep Hole Center,
I see a common door.
At the intersection of which
I rest...*

*One breath for survival
and the second
for gratification.*

*At the rate
desire is being pushed
fulfillment wonders
what mission
must be possible.*

*A little tension released maybe
of that constant migraine headache-
In the manner of instruction
from my physics class,
which I failed twice if not three times,
I envisioned this common door
and pivoted on its hinges.*

*However, the temptation
for rhythmic orgasm
topples my curiosity.
As soon as my indulgence
begins to take over, I let go
to try a little physics experiment.*

*And in no time fulfillment
grabs my legs and sets the hinges straight
as if they were part of my hip bones.
I get up, catch my breath
and feel as if I've been
on a rescue mission.*

DRUG ADDICTS

If I were they
I would sit down
I would look for myself
I would listen to myself
then I would believe in myself.

When they don't know what to do
they sit down and look around.

If they pick the U
they jump Up,
but when they look back
they see the D
they calm Down.
If they pick the G,
they say, "Yeah, that's Good."
When they pick the R,
they say, "Just Right."

But when they put it together,
they miss the D
and say, "Rug,"
then they know
they were wrong.

*If I were they,
I would sleep
for days and nights.
I would eat
all I can.
I would sing
my best song.
I would play
my best instrument.
I would look
at the moon
before I go to bed.
I would look for the sun
the moment I woke up.*

*And then the world
Would believe in me.*

EXCUSES! EXCUSES!

*Many plagues reside in our mind
delaying what needs to be executed.
They stand ready
like a jury for a trial.*

*One by one,
we call on them
as witnesses
to postpone a task,
that must be done.*

*Excuses! Excuses!
Muses of our activities
to justify the nagging
of achievement.*

*They stand tall
like a flagpole.
They stretch wide
like the horizon.*

*Unexpectedly, like a snake
they move
with speed of a tornado,
never to give way.*

SENSELESS DESIRE

*In the space where thoughts have no beginning
and feelings were all around,
I couldn't imagine
the difference between
pleasure and discomfort.*

*A senseless desire,
it seems as if I were
here and there,
all in an instant.
Riding in a train with
the track running
and the train stays frozen.*

*Sitting casually
on a sweet rolling motion-
a sensation within
vibrating outside
in a lopsided progression.*

*I am,
but aware not
that I am.*

*Feeling an indifference
to the space
that I must be...*

BRIDGES

*As a child, I always thought
the horizon was a bridge
between the earth and heaven.
And the sky
could be walked the distance
between the moon and the sun.
Even darkness at night
was a bridge
between today and tomorrow.*

*Bridges, I have come to realize
can be embedded in everything.
And very often I've found
quite a few things can have
more than one bridge.
Consequently, knowing which one to cross
becomes more than a casual walk
or at best a puzzle in the land of confusion.*

For instance, between man and his creator,
consciousness can be harder than steel.
While compassion is a silky woven blanket
fragile as a spider's web.
Then experience came
and opened the gate to wisdom,
a bridge clothed in humility
bounded with emotions that
allow me and my brothers
to rejoice in our differences;
or stand in a daze
like a naked soul waiting for a path
between now and eternity.

BUSINESS TALK

*Whether it's monkey business or not,
business is business.
When you borrow some dollars
to fill your wheelbarrow,
you've got to pay the interest.*

*Even if your nest
is empty;*

*breathe easy
breathe hard
any breath at all
your head is above the water
consequently, you must pay.*

*Pay up or pay out,
pay now or pay later,
you must pay before they slay
your tail and mail it
under your fingernail.*

*Or else, you'll find
a collector
ringing your doorbell
beyond an acceptable decibel.
Consequently, your monologue
will become a stereotypical cliché
and send your breath
into bankruptcy.*

BEING LEGAL

In the realm of legality
society commands
    "Taxes must be paid!"
while nature demands
    "Eat or die!"
Thus leaving the individual
to sit in the dark, naive
as unexposed film
waiting to be engraved
    with the light.

However he who knows
like the wise man
will mingle and dazzle
'til he creates
his own puzzled maze
which the law would never dare
to blow its whistle on.

For the wise man knows
being legal
smokes in the same pipe
as being illegal
except, one
    inhales
while the other
exhales.

BURDENED REALITY

I found the Housekeeper
drunk one day,
and my bedroom
was filled with steam.
Thinking it was a dream,
I called her name.

She replied,
    "Don't disturb the peace,
      I need a moment alone
      to navigate this ship."

Shaken to find
my dream so real,
I eased my burden
with a drink.

Soon I was on that ship
waxing the floor,
dusting the furniture
and making the bed,
like a busy bee working for the queen.
While she sat sipping iced tea,
with a Jackpot Lotto ticket.

Part II: Confrontation

SIBLING RIVALRY

Nothing more than an embryonic division
for the independence of a self reassured—
of the individual in its own territory.

Each having cast his shadow,
in a ceremonial circle
with an emotional display
created an intricate theatrical rendition—
an argument of volcanic bubbles
sweeping the atmosphere—
and then sucking their pride
a larvae of 5000 degrees centigrade
only to form a common ground.

Having settled their score of the division
they rubbed their backs
and pulled each other's ears—
then whispered,

"This shadow has a central core
of light source;
no matter which way we turn
we would knock our heads
and strike a bell
with the same tune over and over again."

DADDY'S WAY

*For Daddy a thought
was a thing
perceived and realized
all at once—
whether she was an ounce
of gold or solid brass.*

*In some kind of way,
the thinker was the skeleton
for which the thought
becomes flesh and blood.*

*However, in time of difficulties
experience demonstrated that
bloody mary
and the red blood cell
were two different things,
while the thought
was yet another
completely foreign to the skeleton.
For whom an alternate motive
with ultimate goal has quite
another purpose.*

*Then, Daddy in his own way
found out that the skeleton may
have the thought
that hates his guts
and loves his butt.*

*However, his realization
in a dreamlike state,
of a thought perceived
came a moment too late.*

*Neither his gut
nor his butt
could stand to put up
with all the thoughts realized.*

*So Daddy was left to rot
in his own way.
While the skeleton set off to go
with all its might and glory.*

*Nonetheless, Daddy in his own way
marched all the way
into the cream of his action
and dissolved into a peaceful urn
while all thoughts perceived
become deceased.*

TRICK OR TREAT

*Dressed in the costume of my other self,
I arrived at the Halloween ball;
looking more like a queen
than the king I thought myself.*

*Caught in this yin-yang dilemma,
while in the darkness of the night
searching for the light in the day,
through the dance rituals
between me and the other person;
she — moving to the slow rhythm of the sax
and me to the fast beat of the drum,
She stepped into my steps.*

*We blew kisses in the air.
Her thoughts departed to the left;
and mine like a butterfly
exited to the right.
Both rose to the occasion
and collided in the mist above our head.*

KISSING DEATH

*I had a kiss with Death
once, twice, too many times.
For every time I saw his face,
I was displaced for the sake
of nurturing the self.*

*Thus, it is for
the great achievement
under grave circumstances-
I dwell on the
circumference of the light
within my mind.*

CONFRONTATION

May Day comes -
  we celebrate
and the confrontation goes on.
Independence Day comes -
  we celebrate
and the war goes on;
come Labor Day -
  we will celebrate.

Some wonder - as most do anyway
why do we hang in there?
For the sweet sorrow we know
we don't clean and dry
for others to wipe their feet.

Part III:
Metamorphosis of Joy

TAKE OFF FROM A RELATIONSHIP

*Through a dimly
lighted sign,
in a landscape
erotically charged
I see my dreams
sprouting like
wild orchids
on Holy ground.*

*Confuse - Diffuse
engrossing thoughts.*

*Like a runner
coming too soon too fast,
equestrian-like
balancing on hind legs.*

*Action - no action
I, a lonely sailor
without a sail
stand still
and watch the scene.*

A FRIENDLY MEMO

*The toast taken at dinner time
was well deserved.
It was not merely
a compliment to the wine;
but more of a gesture for intercourse.*

*Maybe we buried our heads
a little too deep in the glass —
Or, it could have been
some aphrodisiac in the sushi.*

*For whatever it was,
it is now an invisible
connection between us.*

*One small sip on the wine
and we toasted to:
FOREVER FRIENDSHIP —
An ingredient that life
could not do without.*

PAOLINA

*Paolina has a kind of smile;
children playing under
the full moonlight.*

    *The way she smiles
    with her eyes
    flickers like
    fireflies,*

*reminds me of those evenings
with the sky full of stars
when we were burning our energies
chasing crickets by their sounds—
as if we were some kind of
radar detectors
looking for precious germs.*

MYSTERY LADY

Galloping from nowhere
into my somehwhere, she came.
She came for dinner-
ready as a baby
desires his mother's breast
and became the victim
of a few drinks, as I was
after the last course.

I don't even remember
having dessert.
Unless- If it were
the interplay of sex,
a war game - like
for the cause of another.

On the couch, it all began
with instruction coming from behind
I acted.
Why didn't she go?
I thought to myself.

I was ordered to my room with her.
On my bed we sat.
And I showered myself while
she consoled me with a big hug
Then compared me to her kids.

She was a writer I remember;
and she loved the arts.

Why didn't she go?
I thought to myself,
while apologizing
with tears in my eyes.

*But she seemed to have
a better handle of the night
as if she had dealt
with it from the many
lives she lived before,
or from the TV series
we see too often.*

*Throughout the night
she was calm
as a bird perched with her wings
resting gently on her sides.*

*She was concerned not about herself
but more for me-witnessing
my emotional disturbance
an earthquake-like situation.*

*Though I was trying to be strong
she knew well that I was
more scared than she was.
Shaking like a wet chicken
in the cold,
it was like a nightmare.*

*I cannot remember when nor how
in the midst of it all
everything seemed to have faded out,
as an image on the TV screen
gradually disappeared.
The next morning
in the silence of my thoughts,
I observed she was gone
and nothing ever said since.*

SEVEN HEARTS ANGEL

*My baby had seven hearts
and they were all mine.*

*One of pride
so she didn't have
to hide in my shadow.*

*One of lust
so she didn't have
to feel rusted
like a piece of iron
lost in a junk yard.*

*One of reason
so she could bear
the treason
of my impulse
on her senses.*

*One of money
so she could
wine and dine
while I feel
the pain in my spine.*

*One of beauty
so my ego could
be satisfied
In her dignified smile*

*One of justice
so she could squeeze
the sweet experience
and feel rejoiced.
For her eyes
speak to the judge.*

*Yes, my baby
had seven hearts
and they were all mine
so she said.*

FOOLS IN LOVE

Ooh- Ah- 'Mmm—

Close your eyes
and let me touch you.

Ha! Ha! Ha! Ha!

It tickles my breast.

I know;
rest your head on my chest,
feel my heart beat.

It says
"I love you!"
'Mmm I love you too.

You mean
that's what
your heart says.
No, that's the way
I think.

Ah! my heart
feels the love,
your head
thinks the love.

Oh! Yeah...

*I know why,
your head is on my heart.
They think and feel
at the same time.*

'Mmm- Shh! Listen!

*I think they're saying
"It must be love."*

METAMORPHOSIS OF JOY

*She was gentle at first
like a butterfly
in spring time
by the lake under twilight rays.*

*With smiling glossy eyes,
she gazed into my pupils.
She plucked her soft lips
to my defenseless sense of taste-
In an instant she then
diluted my heart
and created her own mold.*

It was ecstasy in exile.

*All the cells in my body
exploded like Macy's fireworks
and the bang was bigger
than Big Bang.*

   BANG

*The place
the time
and the emotion
seem to have created
a communion in heaven.*

*Yet, there were no angels
floating around the stars
to simulate an earthly reality;
drunkards pacing
round and round about bars*

*After a while,
she was yawning for love
only for the dismissal
of some compassionate vibes
overwhelmed with satisfaction.*

*With no recollection of the days before
gone forever with emotion shared;
she clothed herself
with the essence of my existence
my true love's soul.*

*Then in a flash she disappeared;
like a scene in a rear view mirror
as a right turn is taken
under the red light.*

JOY

*Freedom of my senses
to be in the experience
of not existing.*

    This is Joy.

*A myth created
by me - for me
to share with you
as blissful memories
of colors in a fruit basket.*

    This is my Joy.

Part IV:
My Book

NO ORIGIN

As the wind blew - so to say in a curfew
and moved particles to rendez-vous.
So we were there between
the flicks of light; clean-
in the vacuum of mother.

And while she was sleeping
in her state of dreaming,
the shadows of the light were
propelled upon the breeze at night.
Thus she procured us little germs
of a seedless fruit with no sperm.

Nonetheless, she knew of no action
'til she was flashed to see her creation.
Tardily, we little buds swelled to be musers
and united our branches like worshippers
'til we found mother had no origin;
and that sadly forced us to take an aspirin.

A PUZZLE WITHIN

With a do-it-yourself kit
I painted a portrait,
   a self-portrait.
Me-Myself-and I.

First I laid the ground
   all black
In a rectangle.

In the uppermost left corner,
I made a circle
   with the white paint
and said let this be Me.
Perfect as in all perfection.

Next, I placed a dot
   dead center
with the red paint
and said let this be I
one independent magistrate.

Then, I laid my brush down
visualized the tension
between the circle and that dot
Then commanded it
   to be Myself.

TALKING ART

Between the forces of creativity:
the melody of my sound reigns supreme.
It runs through your spine
and juggles your every bone.

The voices in my poems
echo through your ears
and settle upon your heart-
there become your emotions.

The colors of my palette,
they penetrate through
your pupils
there they remain forever.

RIGHT OF PURPOSE #1

*There are those who carry
their head on their shoulders
high in disguise of a proud hero
on the battlefront.*

*There are those who drag
their feet beneath their bottom;
low and slow
with no desire for a destination.*

*For each it is a load
that must be taken
along the road,
in any way comfort ease.*

*While others seem to balance
the two and thrust them effortlessly
in the direction of a gentle breeze;
then at any time can change their
action with a simple sneeze.*

*It seems that for them
the direction
is in the action.
And the action is in the loading
while the loading is in the*

RITE OF PURPOSE.

RIGHT OF PURPOSE #2

*There are those who dance
by the fire in a ritualistic manner,
for a chance to chase
the Spirit away.*

*There are those who dance
and bathe in bubble bath,
then, go into a trance
with the hope of lancing
the Spirit into their circle.*

*For everyone, in a ritualistic manner
has a purpose for which he carries a banner.*

*Hence, there are those who eat
to starve the Spirit
'til it becomes a fatless beacon
and there are those who eat
to feed the Spirit
into a healthy cow.*

*As in the observance of law and order
for each action there is a reaction,
for each motion there is a momentum.*

*However, in the RITE OF PURPOSE
it's merely a matter
of intention within condition.*

AN ENDLESS WALK

*Many walks a life has
for one to travel
in endless direction.
Some take a walk
at night in their dreams
and have no fear
of demons at crossroads.
Others walk under the sun,
sweating salty greasy
drips of hard suffering
day's work for living,
while wondering
if the fortunate turn
is against their shadow.*

Walk - Walk - Walk

*In a marching band style
I shall conquer
on the other side
of the bridge.*

Walk - Walk - Walk

*Like lovers strolling
in the spring season
while listening
to the birds singing
and sniffing the aroma
of budding flowers*

*I walk, I walk, I walk
all the walks of life
to find a new horizon
with no dimension.*

BEYOND THE HORIZON

*Slowly, shiny rocks do light
brighter than those at night.*

Treasure of tomorrow is in the sea.

*It sits like a crab beneath the rocks,
patiently waiting.*

*Suddenly two arrows
drove into my eyes
and left only tea.*

*Silently, I sat like a pile of socks,
then sweetly, in my corner,
the birds sang.
My legs were tight
as if they were in stocks.
I could not dance, or sing,
so I banged.*

*I tried again,
my hands went through a net.
joyfully, I cried,*

"MY LORD, THIS IS MY PET."

TRUTH 101

Wishing wishes
with wishbones
hanging by my neck,
I am soon to find
  my wish.

A V-neck brace

  squeezing
my tongue out-
sweeping every
street corner
  for the lies
within my wish.

A PENSIVE MOMENT

*Hold the thought of being loved
by someone unknown to you.
One who has power to lower
your being into another
world yet unknown to you.*

*That someone may choose
to elevate your consciousness
into a higher realm of life
which then turns your
present life into a dream.*

*Can you then chance the risk
of kicking your legs like a frog —
which may then sabotage that one
in an entourage of steaming
love without compassion.*

*What reason then would he
have to give you tender loving care.
As if you were the only
soul mate one being loved —*

*Having held this thought
long enough into your
tiny net of spider's web,
you must entrust into
your mind the realization
that to capitalize on knowing
that someone is your most
profitable route.*

*In turn render you portable
as an amphibiant Soul
to an unknown world below;
or to the highest realm
of consciousness in the center
of an orgasmic eruption;
echoing the sound of*

A--U---M---

ON AND ON

*When the clock stops
will we go on living?
For there'll be no hours
to give us a day- to shave
the unwanted hair of ours*

*When the clock stops
will we go on living?
For there'll be no days
to give us a year- to count
the unwanted eggs we lay.*

*When the clock stops
Will we go on and on?
For there'll be
no hours to swing
and sing for love
no days to pray
and pay our dues
no years to sow
and grow our seeds.*

*When the clock stops
Or will the clock stop.
Oh! No!*

MY BOOK

*Some kids start reading
with their ABC's
and all the in between,
before they get to their XYZ's.*

*Then they'll graduate
from sentences, paragraphs
to chapters — before they complete
a whole book.*

*I wasn't like that;
I started with the Good Book
and taking it page by page.*

No, I wasn't in a rage.

*You could say I was
a Book Worm.*

*I chewed those pages
dozens by the second.*

What did I know?

*My father left that big book
under my pillow
long before 12 equals 1*

*Somehow I imagined,
or was it a dream?
I had to learn its contents
by osmosis-
but Daddy thought that
putting the book
beneath my head
would keep evil spirits
from my sleep.

I slept all right.
After taking those pages
dozens by the second.
A funny thing happened though
when 12 equaled 1 —
I got slower.

By the time 12 equaled 24 over 12
it was time for those ABC's.
Then I had no choice
but to start reading
instead of dreaming.*

*I read 'til one day
that Book started
arguing with me.
I argued back and got angry.
So angry I didn't want
to hear what it had to say.
However, wherever I go
whatever I do
it kept talking*

*And by the time
12 equaled 396 over 12
I realized the value of
that Good Book was
the sum total of its pages
less its cover multiplied
by how much it had
enlarged my mind to the Universe.*

ABOUT THE AUTHOR

ALBERT DÉPAS, a multi-media artist and poet was born in Port-Au-Prince, Haiti. He came to the United States at the age of fifteen, at which time his studies of the arts began with his father—also a fine artist of multi-media. Albert then continued his studies at the Brooklyn Museum Art School and at City College, where he studied fine arts and architecture. He expresses himself primarily with oil on canvas, oil-pastel and photography.

He has read his poetry throughout New York City, and his artworks have been exhibited in the City as well. He is also the founder and editor of *Show & Tell*, a publication for the visual arts and poetry.

Cover Painting: *Yin-Yang Dilemma,* oil on canvas, 18" x 24".